# No More Strangers Now

A Melanie Kroupa Book

# No More

# Strangers Now

## YOUNG VOICES FROM A
## NEW SOUTH AFRICA

### INTERVIEWS BY TIM MCKEE

### PHOTOGRAPHS BY ANNE BLACKSHAW

### FOREWORD BY ARCHBISHOP DESMOND TUTU

DORLING KINDERSLEY PUBLISHING, INC.

**A note on the language used in this book:** In the short introductions that precede each story, we have referred to South Africa's different ethnic groups individually wherever possible, using the terms *whites*, *Africans*, *Coloureds*, and *Indians*. There are places, however, where we use the term *black* to describe collectively all those oppressed under apartheid, as in the "black resistance movement" or "the treatment of blacks." The teens themselves, however, often use the term *black* to refer specifically to Africans.

A Melanie Kroupa Book
Dorling Kindersley Publishing, Inc.
95 Madison Avenue
New York, New York 10016

Visit us on the World Wide Web at http://www.dk.com

Foreword copyright © 1998 by Archbishop Desmond Tutu
Text copyright © 1998 by Timothy Saunders McKee
Photographs copyright © 1998 by Anne Cecelia Blackshaw

Grateful acknowledgement is made to Ad Donker Publishers and Mongane Wally Serote for permission to reprint the excerpts from the poem "No More Strangers" by Mongane Wally Serote. Copyright held by Mongane Wally Serote.

*Library of Congress Cataloging-in-Publication Data*

No more strangers now : young voices from a new South Africa / interviews by Tim McKee ; with photographs by Anne Blackshaw.
    p.   cm.
    Contents: Ricardo Thando Tollie — Leandra Jansen van Vuuren — Nithinia Martin — Nomfundo Mhlana — Michael Njova — Vuyiswa Mbambisa — Mark Abrahamson — Bandile Mashinini — Pfano Takalani — Lebogang Maile — Nonhlanhla Mavundla — Lavendhri Pillay.
    Summary: In their own words, a variety of teenagers from South Africa talk about their years growing up under apartheid, and about the changes now occurring in their country.
    ISBN 0-7894-2524-6 (hc) / 0-7894-2663-3 (pb)
    1. South Africa — Race relations — Juvenile literature. 2. South Africa — Politics and government — 1994 — Juvenile literature. 3. South Africa — Social conditions — 1961 — Juvenile literature. [1. South Africa — Race relations — Personal narratives. 2. South Africa — Social conditions — 1961 — Personal narratives. 3. Blackshaw, Anne, ill.] I. McKee, Tim.
DT1974N66  1998                              97-47293
968'.00496—dc21                                CIP
                                                                     AC

Book design by Chris Hammill Paul.
The text of this book is set in 14 point Centaur.
Printed and bound in U.S.A.

First Paperback Edition, 2000
10  9  8  7  6  5  4  3  2  1

*For Connie, Khutso, and Kabelo*

# ACKNOWLEDGMENTS

There were many people who made this book possible. We are deeply grateful for the help of the many community organizers and local activists who spent countless hours with us setting up, overseeing, and sometimes translating interviews. They allowed us to reach young people we would never have found on our own, and their enthusiasm for this project consistently refueled our spirits. They include: Anni Hennop, Barry M'bele, Lesley Osler, Manelisi Nelani, Moira Simpson, Adele Pillay, David Hiscock, Maxwell Nkala, Irene and Rother Mashamba, Sister Elizabeth Mokoena, and Dominica Msomi.

The folks at People Opposing Women Abuse (POWA) and Barnato Park High School, where we worked, allowed us flexibility to travel the country in pursuit of these stories and provided unconditional support when we returned back home to Johannesburg. We are lucky to have been part of these communities. At Barnato Park, special thanks go to Agnes Nugent, the students of Iso Labantu, Murray Hofmeyr, Laura Macris, and Eric and Naomi Molobi.

Johnathan Dorfman, Stevan Buxt, and Lindsey and Ned Breslin generously provided computers when we needed them. Sally and Cathy Shackleton provided moral and administrative support throughout the process.

Danny Hoffman spent many hours examining negatives and contact sheets and served both as mentor and informal photo editor. Tsheko Kabasia and everyone at the Market Theatre Photographers' Workshop provided a dynamic darkroom environment for the developing and printing of these photographs. And thanks to Bill Blackshaw, whose passion for photography helped stir the same in his daughter.

Mongane Wally Serote and Ad Donker Publishers granted permission to use parts of Mr. Serote's poem "No More Strangers" for the opening poem and title of the book. For his opening remarks in the Foreword, we are deeply grateful to Archbishop Desmond Tutu and his assistant, Lavinia Browne.

Once back in the United States we relied on many people for editing suggestions on our manuscript and photos. Doris McKee, Fred Kuretski, Jay Blackshaw, and Amy Blackshaw all gave us constructive criticism and support in the crucial last stages of the process. Educators Greg Feldmeth, Jody Stefansson, and Ruth Lavagnino led us to students at Marshall High School and Polytechnic School who gave us straightforward feedback on the first draft of the book.

Other family members provided additional assistance. John Blackshaw and Jennifer McKee gave us excellent legal advice when we needed it, and Bill and Julie Blackshaw helped turn a dilapidated shed into a wonderful darkroom for final printing of the photographs. Thanks to the rest of our families for their ongoing support. Many thanks also to our friends in both the United States and South Africa for consistent encouragement along the way.

Our editor, Melanie Kroupa, recognized early on the value of telling these stories. She provided us with invaluable support, feedback, and vision in shaping the manuscript and photographs. Hazel Rochman also provided inspiration, sharing in the initial brainstorming session that sparked the idea and reading pieces of the stories as they first came together. We also thank Chris Paul for her terrific design and everyone else at DK Ink.

Finally, most of the credit goes to the teenagers and families who allowed us such an intimate view into their lives. They, more than anyone else, were our teachers and guides on this journey. Their warmth and generosity of spirit were incredible. ━

# FOREWORD

This is an important and timely book. The stories that unfold here come from all over South Africa and weave a fabric of this nation's troubled history and its long path to freedom. Told in the resonant voices of twelve young South Africans, they speak not only of the great suffering and pain experienced under the insanity of apartheid but also of the triumph of will that marked our recent transition to democracy and of the limitless possibilities of our future.

And yet the reach of these stories extends beyond the borders of South Africa; in addressing universal themes like poverty, racism, faith, and reconciliation, they carry relevance for all the world's people.

In South Africa we are learning to heal through the telling of stories like these, for it is only through telling that we heal; it is only through revealing the heart's darkest crevices that we can begin to understand, to forgive, and to move forward.

And we are moving forward. After years of mistrust we are beginning to open our hearts and minds to one another; we are learning to see the humanity that lives in each one of us. Through the voices of these young people and the photographs that bring them to life, this book represents one more bridge in this historic process. ━

*Archbishop Desmond Tutu*

ZIMBABWE

MOZAMBIQUE

BOTSWANA

Mukula ○

Pietersburg ○

Potgietersrus ○

Pretoria ○

NAMIBIA

Johannesburg ●
Soweto
Alexandra
Westbury
Yeoville
Benoni

Mbabane ○

SWAZILAND

Kimberley ○

Bloemfontein ○

Maseru ○

LESOTHO

Pietermaritzburg ○

Durban ○

*Orange River*

*Orange River*

ATLANTIC OCEAN

Grootfontein ○

Khayelisha ○ ○ Port Shepstone

INDIAN OCEAN

Cape Town ●
Rondebosch
Vrygrond

Port Elizabeth ○

~ SOUTH AFRICA ~

# INTRODUCTION

SOUTH AFRICA TODAY is a nation bursting with the spirit of a revolution victorious. After centuries of resistance, the election of President Nelson Mandela in 1994 signaled the end of apartheid, the infamous system of racial segregation by which the country's white minority had enjoyed privilege and freedom while denying the black majority its most basic human rights. In Yeoville, Johannesburg, where we lived in 1996 and 1997, Tim as a high school teacher and Anne as a community organizer, change seemed to resonate from every corner. The nation's new flag hung in doorways and from car windows, and black and white children alike were singing the new national anthem, *"Nkosi Sikelel' iAfrika,"* a hauntingly beautiful song with a long history as a resistance anthem.

Beyond such visual and symbolic signs of reconciliation, however, South Africa remains a country bitterly divided along racial lines. Apartheid, literally defined as "apartness," preached a gospel of separation that ran so deep that communities of different colors still seem no closer to understanding or even knowing each other. The majority of black South Africans still live in urban matchbox houses or rural mud huts, while most whites continue to live in spacious homes fitted with intricate alarm systems and the latest appliances. Many black classrooms lack books, windows, and even chalk, whereas white schools have everything from computers to well-manicured playing fields. The nation's peoples still live in very different worlds.

Yet most South Africans seem to share an almost uncanny confidence that the miracle of 1994 will not be fleeting and that a stable, vibrant nation will emerge. Much of their hope rests with the nation's young people who, despite being born and raised during apartheid, are coming of age in a time of new beginnings and hope. All of the young people you will meet in this book experienced apartheid differently, but they share an enthusiasm for their futures and a belief that they can together create a more equal society. Through their stories, the agony of South Africa's past and its challenges for the present and future become clear. As Mark Abrahamson, one of the teenagers, says, "We're the generation that's the bridge from the previous South Africa to a new one."

TO UNDERSTAND the complicated climate in South Africa today, it is essential to understand the country's long and troubled history. Although apartheid officially began in 1948, its roots go back to 1652, when Dutch settlers first landed in Cape Town to establish a stopping-off point for ships sailing around the southern tip of Africa on their way to the Far East. Over the next few decades the number of whites increased as settlers from France and Germany arrived. Through intermarriage the Dutch and the new Europeans slowly became one distinct culture with its own language; they became Afrikaners, which in the Afrikaans language simply means "Africans."

But Afrikaners did not "discover" a new land; for thousands of years indigenous Africans had been living throughout the area. To ensure their dominance, Afrikaners displaced the way of life of native inhabitants by forcing many of them into servitude and off their family lands. They also imported slaves from places known today as Malaysia, Indonesia, Sri Lanka, and Madagascar. They prohibited Africans and slaves from taking part in the running of the colony, including the mixed-race Coloureds, who emerged when settlers intermingled with native and slave populations.

This power structure changed significantly in 1795 when Great Britain wrested control of the Cape Colony from the Dutch. The British outlawed slavery in the colony in 1834, infuriating the Afrikaners who had become dependent on free labor. In ox-drawn wagons, many Afrikaners traveled eastward to escape British control, convinced the land they found was theirs to take. Battles over land erupted between the Afrikaners and the Africans they met during these expansions. Despite fierce resistance, the Africans were finally defeated by the modern weapons Afrikaners used against them. In the meantime, English settlers began bringing indentured servants from India to work on sugar plantations.

Over the ensuing decades the Afrikaner and English settlers, who together made up only 14 percent of the population, put aside their differences to maintain power over the Coloureds, Indians, and Africans. In 1948 the Afrikaner-controlled National party took over the government and, aiming to strengthen further the white minority's grip, instituted its policy of apartheid. Apartheid was founded on the belief that racial mixing was immoral and that each race therefore should be separated from the others. An African and a white could not marry; a Coloured and an Indian could not live in the same neighborhood; a white and an Indian could not sit in the same classroom.

But the white founders of apartheid never intended to create a separate and equal society; because they believed they were superior to the other races and needed to maintain control, they deliberately created a separate and unequal society in which the lighter your skin, the more benefits you received. The result was a society not only segregated but stratified. While whites received top-notch educations, lived in plush suburbs, and held the most powerful jobs, Indians, Coloureds, and Africans attended under-funded schools, lived in neglected townships outside the cities, and could take only the jobs that whites allowed them, most often as manual laborers and domestic workers. Apartheid also created inequalities within South Africa's nonwhite, or black, populations: Africans, perceived as the most inferior citizens, attended the worst schools and held the lowest jobs, while Indians and Coloureds, seen as inferior to whites but superior to Africans, were slightly better off.

Yet in the face of these racist policies a profound spirit of resistance thrived. Spearheaded by the African National Congress (ANC), Africans, Coloureds, Indians, and some whites worked together to establish an effective grassroots protest movement. But progress came slowly; by separating South Africans so completely, apartheid made it difficult for activists to unite against the system. Furthermore, the apartheid government went to great lengths to silence critics, banning anti-apartheid organizations, censoring opposition newspapers, and murdering, torturing, and arresting anti-apartheid leaders it branded dangerous terrorists. For their own safety many activists fled South Africa, settling in exile in countries like Angola, Tanzania, the Soviet Union, and the United Kingdom, where they continued to fight apartheid from the outside. They, together with their colleagues who remained either imprisoned or "underground" in South Africa, relentlessly pursued their vision of a multiracial democracy until 1994, when Nelson Mandela took office as the nation's first democratically elected president.

◤ IN SEEKING THESE STORIES we spent roughly ten months speaking with more than sixty-five teenagers from all over the country about their lives. We walked down dusty paths to remote villages, clunked along potholed roads to sprawling townships, and whizzed down modern highways to elegant suburbs. We attended the largest indoor church in South Africa, watched the chase and slaughter of a ceremonial chicken, and were granted an audience with a traditional African chief at his royal residence. We chose the twelve teens you will meet here not only because they came from a wide range of social, economic, ethnic, and geographic backgrounds, but also because they were able to speak openly about their experiences under apartheid and their attempts to carve out a role for themselves in the new South Africa. Most of the interviews were conducted in English, but occasionally a translator was needed to interview teens who spoke another one of South Africa's eleven official languages. The stories are all in the teenagers' own words, except when a slight modification was needed for clarification.

We did our best to immerse ourselves in the lives of these twelve teens, sometimes at the risk of becoming nuisances. With our camera and tape recorder in hand, we spent several days following them everywhere, from the breakfast table to their walks to school, from their first-period classes to their recesses. We ate meals with their families, sat down on their beds, stood inside their classrooms, and, by the end, left as friends. Although many of the teens were surprised by what they saw as an unwarranted amount of attention ("What's so important about me?" one asked), they and their families all generously opened their homes, communities, and lives to us.

It would be easy to hear the optimism and hope of these stories and think that the future of South Africa is secure. In fact, the determination and spirit of the teens we interviewed became so infectious that at times we felt almost giddy with the sense that the greatest hurdles had been overcome. But as we continued to drive down dirt roads to communities without plumbing, electricity, and adequate schools, we were reminded again and again that perhaps the hardest work still lies ahead.

What we learned on our journey more than anything, however, is that the human spirit is more powerful than any force that tries to suppress it. Africans call this *ubuntu*, which Archbishop Desmond Tutu has defined as "the essence of being human.... It embraces compassion and toughness. It recognizes that my humanity is bound up in yours, for we can only be human together." Regardless of their backgrounds and the challenges they face, these teenagers share a will to reveal this humanity, to overcome biases, to heal from wounds, and to move proudly forward. In this pursuit we're all more partners than strangers.

*Tim McKee*

*Anne Blackshaw*

*It were us, it is us*

*the children of Soweto*

*langa, kagiso, alexandra, gugulethu and nyanga*

*us*

*a people with a long history of resistance*

*us*

*who will dare the mighty*

*for it is freedom, only freedom which can quench*

*our thirst——*

*we did learn from terror that it is us who will*

*seize history*

*our freedom.*

*. . . It were us it is us*

*who were taught by history*

*that terror before the will of the people*

*is like a sheep in the mouth of a crocodile*

*here we go again*

*we have learnt from so many cruel nights*
*that oppressors are guilty forever*
*and we know that we will move.*

*it will be the trees, the mountains*
*it will be the silence of the karoo and its heat*
*it will be the song of our rivers*
*moving, us one with them*
*moving*
*the night giving us sanctuaries*
*the day witness but silent*
*it will be us*
*steel-taut to fetch freedom*
*and—*
*we will tell freedom*
*we are no more strangers now.*

*Mongane Wally Serote*
*from the poem "No More Strangers"*

*One of the cornerstones of apartheid was the Group Areas Act of 1950, which segregated South African towns and cities by giving whites free access to city centers and surrounding suburbs while forcing Africans, Indians, and Coloureds to live in separate townships.*

*But not all blacks obeyed this law. Frustrated by overcrowding in the townships, many chose to build their own shacks in empty spaces around city perimeters. The government initially responded by destroying these "squatter camps" with bulldozers. Over time, however, these camps became too large and numerous to control. The government finally allowed the camps to grow unchecked but never provided any of the basic services needed for human existence. The result was a sprawling mass of tin shacks nestled between open sewers and rocky paths that served as roads.*

*Sixteen-year-old Ricardo Thando Tollie lives in a small tin shack in Vrygrond (Free Ground), one of the oldest squatter camps outside Cape Town.*

## OUT OF THE SHACKS
# Ricardo Thando Tollie

◤ I'VE LIVED IN A SHACK my whole life. It's been very difficult to grow up in a place like this because the community has nothing. People don't have proper houses, don't have toilets. When it's raining, it's leaking everywhere in our shack; you have to try and sleep in places the rain won't reach you. As kids we didn't have many toys, so we would take old car tires and push them along with sticks or make some kites with paper. Sometimes a guy would steal a bike from somewhere else; then he would come by and offer it to us. If we had any money, we'd buy it, and then we'd have to change the way it looked. That's how we got things.

✉ Ricardo and his brothers and sisters have grown up with few luxuries. "My mom makes tea and cleans classrooms at a junior school, and she must pay for five kids with her salary as a tea girl."

We didn't have a school in Vrygrond, so my parents sent me to a nearby school in a Coloured township. In the mornings I would make a fire to heat up the iron, and sometimes the fire would make the iron dirty, so I'd end up with a black mark on my white shirt. Then I'd leave for school at half past six, walk for an hour and a half, and get to school with my hair not clean, my hair not combed.

At school I was the only black and the only kid from Vrygrond, and the kids were always putting me down. They would say, "Ha! You're living in the shacks in that *kaffir* [South African equivalent of *nigger*] place! You're poor! You live in the sewer! You can't stay with us in this

Ricardo is concerned about his younger brother Albert's future. "When I get a good job, I will help send my brother to school so he doesn't end up like my older sisters, who are at home, unemployed."

school!" I didn't have a lot of friends, and in class and at break I was always by myself. I stopped saying that I stayed in Vrygrond because I was too embarrassed.

But when I was about twelve, I was seeing many black people fighting against apartheid, and I began to realize, It's because of apartheid, that's why we don't have proper houses! Why must I hide the place that I live in? I realized that black people came to Vrygrond because the whites wanted the blacks to work for them but then wouldn't

▧ Ricardo is a well-known figure around Vrygrond. "My friends and I want to call meetings with people and decide what we want to work on," he says. "We want to have a civic center with basketball courts, because we don't have such things."

allow us to live next to them in their white areas. So I started telling the kids at school that I lived in Vrygrond, and if they laughed, I would ask them, "Why are you laughing? I can't help it if I stay in shacks like this!"

At this age I was getting cross at apartheid and blaming the white people, because I saw that apartheid put the white man up there, the Coloured in the middle, and the black man down here. I thought that maybe I could have lived like whites if they didn't treat us the way they did in apartheid.

Even now a white boy who's sixteen like me has many things that I don't have. He will wake up and his servant has already made breakfast, and he can eat it in bed. But me, I must wake up at five o' clock to go to the bush and fetch some wood so I can make a fire to heat up water for tea and washing. At school he has computers, classes with heaters, everything he wants. But at our school we don't even have one computer, and our windows are broken and it's cold inside.

When I see whites in their big houses, I still get jealous and angry. I hope the white kids will come and see how we live in Vrygrond. They don't know there are such places in Cape Town; it's not on a map, and it will never be on TV. They need to know the troubles we still have

The shacks in Vrygrond are made from sheets of zinc and aluminum, and pieces of plastic and wood. "I want to tell whites, 'You must live in this little house for a year.' Then you will see, you will come to us every day and say, 'No, I want my house back. It's too cold in this shack.'"

Ricardo and his brother often have to repair their family's fence by reconnecting the long pieces of tin that separate when Cape Town's strong winter winds arrive. "If you do your work, then your shack can be a home. But people here, they want real houses, they don't want to live like this."

here and need to know how their fathers and grandfathers treated our people before. They must see that most people are not free like them.

But things are beginning to improve for us. For so long we didn't have electricity or telephones, but the new ANC government cares about our people and is putting those things in Vrygrond now. And we are going to have our own houses soon. Some people want houses now. They think that Mandela will fix everything wrong from the past, but he can't do everything at one time. We just have to wait.

In the meantime, I still go to a Coloured school, but now it's mixed with more blacks, and I'm accepted, I have many friends. I am studying hard because I now have chances my parents did not have. They had to go work for the *baas* [the white boss], but for me the picture has changed; if I work hard, I can finish high school and then study further with accounting. I can sit in an office, drive my own car. When I was younger, I was drinking and smoking because my friends and I didn't have hope; drinking helped us forget about things. My mother would shout at me, "You're not taking note of your schoolbooks!" But now I've stopped doing those things, and my old friends even tell me I will get crazy from studying so much. I just tell them, "Okay, we'll see when I'm done."

If I make some money when I finish school, the first thing I will do is build my mother a house because always that's what she wanted. We must build the house in Vrygrond because our roots are here, everything we do is here. The people of Vrygrond have struggled together, fought together, done everything together. We worry about each other. If your house is burning, everybody is going to go out and help you build your house again. And they'll give you food and let you sleep at their house while you build it. People say this is a squatter camp, but to me it's like any other place, because we people living here are the same as other people. God created all of us, and that's how we must see each other.

*Most white schools, churches, and communities supported apartheid's notion that black South Africans were inferior to whites. Now that South Africans are allowed to mix freely, many whites are beginning to realize how shallow and racist their perceptions of Africans were. But biases still run deep, especially in South Africa's small rural towns, where segregation and mistrust remain the norm.*

*Fifteen-year-old Leandra Jansen van Vuuren comes from one such town, Potgietersrus, tucked amid white farms in the northern part of the country. Potgietersrus was the subject of worldwide attention in 1996, when white parents blocked a public elementary school's entrance to keep black pupils from attending.*

## LEARNING TO SEE
# Leandra Jansen van Vuuren

WHEN I WAS SMALL I was told I had to stay away from black people because they were almost like animals: They were dangerous; they could kill you. I used to overhear my aunt telling my mother that blacks were going to take over our houses, kill the women and children and that the men were not allowed to leave their children and wives at home. My father had a .22 rifle, and he said, "Okay, my darling, if they come into our house, we'll just kill them."

My father raises chickens and pigs on our farm, and I used to go with him when he'd sell them in the black townships. I'd see black kids there, but I'd just walk away from them. It was almost like, "No, you

 Leandra spends the week living at school but returns home to her family's farm on weekends. "My father was always a farmer, and my family loves this land."

can stay there and I'll stay here. You must be away from me." I'd say things like, "Hey, look at the *kaffir!*" I thought it was just a way to describe a black person; I didn't know then that it wasn't nice. The white kids around me also grew up on farms, and they never mixed with blacks either.

To me it just seemed that blacks and whites were in different places. At school and church there were only whites; they didn't tell us about the way blacks lived. I didn't know what was happening to black people, that things were unfair. They taught us about all the dead Afrikaners that the blacks had killed, to be proud of the places where

Afrikaners died for us, and that Afrikaners had done good things for South Africa.

So when I heard that apartheid was going away, I hated it. I thought, Why must they move near us, why must they take our land over, why must they mix with us? When I'd visit my nephew near Pretoria and we'd see black kids who had moved close, we'd chase them on bikes, and we'd yell, "Hey, why are you coming here?"

Leandra often helps take care of her family's pigs, the Jansen van Vuurens' main source of income.

 Leandra's stay at a weekend camp with others of different races changed her in many ways. "When I was little, people in my community always told me black people were dangerous, and I believed them," she says. "But at camp we began to learn that we are able to trust one another."

Even last year, when black kids first tried to come to our school, I saw white parents who stood outside the gates and tried to stop them from coming. I kind of agreed with them, like, why can't the blacks stay in their own schools? And when the blacks did come in, the white kids said, "They're a bunch of idiots; they can't even write." I said it as well.

I began to change a bit when our church began to have black people in it. I mean, if you love God, you love God. The Bible says that God inspired the people to rise in all nations. Everybody should be welcome in the church, and I saw that those churches that didn't want to let blacks in were not right.

The thing that changed me most was going to a weekend camp with black kids and Indians. When I first came to the camp, all the kids were eating, and they said, "Come, come, sit by us." I first felt a bit out with the black ones, and the first night I thought I had to be careful. But then we began to play cricket and soccer, and I saw that Indians, whites, and blacks, all the colors, were playing together.

We also had to find a "buddy" who was different from us, and I found a black girl. Her hair felt a bit tough, not the same as ours, not fine. Her eyes were brown, and when she would talk, they'd go so big like she had a fright. She talked louder than me and had different traditions, but in other ways we were the same. She wore the same kind of clothes as me, long pants and a normal T-shirt. She was a Christian, too.

I will keep in touch with all the friends I made at camp. It's better to have a friend than to have no friend, even if that person looks different from me. My buddy lives in a township, and if she asks me over, I'll go. When I get together with her, we're going to play, of course. But I'd also like to learn some things from her culture, like dance. And I'd like to learn her language. People always like you more if you can speak their language.

It's strange that just by eating with someone or going to church with someone, you can begin to see them. Earlier this year before I went to camp, I saw shacks in the city where black people were living, and I laughed. But you know, now I'm learning more, and I see that if we had to live in that, we wouldn't laugh, we wouldn't think it was a joke. I used to think it was all right when I'd see stories on TV about how white policemen used to hit black people. But now I see they are also human beings, and they need a chance to live. After fourteen

▼ Leandra is learning to shed her biases and get to know black students, who began to attend her school in 1996. "The other kids might tease me for being friends with blacks, but I'm not going to pay them any mind. I feel like a pressure has gone off my shoulders."

years of not mixing very much, just two days made me start to think differently.

At first I don't think my father is going to like to hear that I'm playing with blacks because he's not very used to it. But I think you can teach your parents that it's not right to be racist against other people. My father will be glad after I explain it to him because I will tell him that it's time to learn how to make friends, because if we don't have that, what are we going to do?

Most of the kids at school don't know what I've learned. If a black girl comes close, a lot of them will just move away. I can see that they are afraid to mix; I know this because I was afraid, too. But I've made a new beginning, and I think it's important now to try and change things at my school. The message I want to give is that everyone must learn to respect one another and that will make life far easier. Apartheid gave us a very bad image of the blacks; it didn't tell us the truth. That is what we have to change, so that we see them as they really are, not what we think they are. If we don't respect them, we won't ever have a day when we say, "We're sorry, we were blind."

*The Population Registration Act of 1950 classified all South Africans by race so that the government could ensure that each citizen was in his or her proper place on the apartheid ladder.*

*In the middle of this racial caste system were Coloureds, who constitute 9 percent of South Africa's population. Like Africans, Coloureds were forced to live in townships, accept inferior education, and take only low-paying jobs. But Coloureds were also placed one rung above Africans, living in communities and attending schools with slightly better resources than their African counterparts.*

*Eighteen-year-old Nithinia Martin lives in Westbury, a Coloured township in Johannesburg located between the white suburb of Westdene and the African township of Soweto.*

## STUCK IN THE MIDDLE

# Nithinia Martin

◥ AS A COLOURED, apartheid taught me basically that I'm better than blacks but that I can never be white. We were on the fence, stuck in the middle.

Whites were sly. They gave Coloureds a bit higher position than blacks and told us that we're better than them. They must have feared that if we got to know blacks and saw the good in them, then we might interact and start becoming one, and that united, we might have destroyed the whole system. Like in the last elections, most Coloureds voted for Mandela, and see he won, because we stood together.

So I grew up thinking just like the apartheid government wanted

 Nithinia lives in a four-room house with her grandmother, aunts, and eight cousins. She and her cousins have all lost their fathers to the gang violence that infests Westbury. "Sometimes I get jealous when I hear men tell their kids, 'Daddy loves you.' If they can hear that, why didn't we get the chance to, just once?"

me to. Even though I had black relatives, I was always taught to curse my own blackness because it prevented me from being white. I was angry about my parts that were black; I grew my hair long and used a hair relaxer to make it thin, so that I would not look like a black person. And I saw whites as superior. Whenever I had contact with them, they were dressed well and drove nice cars. When I saw the way whites were portrayed on TV, I thought, That's the ideal way of living. I'd always say to myself, If only my hair was straight and I had blue eyes, I'd be white.

I remember once my aunt brought me and my cousins three dolls. My one cousin is very dark in complexion, my other cousin is fair, and I'm in the middle. One of the dolls was black, and the other two were white. So we started arguing, "Who's gonna take the black doll? I'm not taking it!" Afterward my dark cousin took it, but she was weeping the whole time, and she said, "It's because I'm darker—that's why you're giving me the black doll." I would admire the white doll I got and think, This is the way I should have looked, if only. . .

⬧ Nithinia takes a bus to church every Sunday morning. "It's a place where people get along, where color is not of prime importance," she says. "I'm learning to look not skin deep but to the bottom of who people are."

Nithinia and her cousin often talk on the back porch when their house gets too crowded. "We may be struggling, but we always give each other love."

It was all really confusing to me. On the one hand, I admired whites, and on the other, I sort of hated them because I knew they were oppressing us. Apartheid made it so that whites who didn't even finish school could get proper jobs, while blacks and Coloureds who *had* finished school couldn't. I think that's why my father got involved in gangs. He didn't finish school, and he was Coloured, so it was almost impossible to find work. With gangs he could make a living.

When I was about three or four years old, my father got arrested for the murder of another gangster, even though people say he didn't do it. He was in jail for a few years, and then he got sentenced to death. I remember visiting him in prison and my grandmother telling me to say good-bye because I wouldn't see him again. My eyes were watering because I wanted to cry, but I just said good-bye. That's the only way I can remember my father, sitting behind a glass. I can remember seeing tears in his eyes, just looking at me, staring at me, saying nothing.

After my dad died, two of his brothers were also killed because of

Through a youth group at her church, Nithinia is getting to know teenagers from different backgrounds. "Before I was taught only the differences between us, but now I'm seeing the links, too."

 While her grandmother irons neighbors' clothes for extra income, Nithinia keeps her company by reading aloud from the Bible.

the gangs. I lived with his mother, my granny, because my parents were never married and I didn't know my mom then. My granny started selling drugs because when her sons died, there wasn't enough money for all of us to live on. Drug addicts would come to my granny and sell their gold watches, wedding bands, furniture, expensive things, just for a few pills. I'd sell to people when they'd come to the house. I saw how those drugs would destroy people, destroy families. But I sold anyway, because I thought I was helping my family and it was the right thing to do. When the police would come, my gran would give us kids the drugs to keep because the police wouldn't search us. I'd keep them in my hands or shove them in my socks. I'd be so scared.

Last year my granny finally decided she was causing too much pain and stopped selling drugs. Now gangs are the main salesman. Gangs have gotten worse here since my dad's days. Before, they fought only with stones and knives, but now everyone has guns. Westbury is so violent now; you don't know where to walk or when you might get killed. Whatever the gangsters do, nobody does nothing about it because people are too scared to say anything.

There are so many guys involved in drugs and gangs because there's no sense of hope in our community; it's very dim. In a way I feel we Coloureds are still stuck in the middle. Now it's almost like everything's just the opposite. Before it was white, now it's black, but it's like we Coloureds aren't black enough now, just like we weren't white enough before. We're getting passed over in things like affirmative action, even though we stood by blacks before.

I want to get out of Westbury very badly. I'd say I've lost about ten family members or friends to the gangs, and I feel doomed in this place. You sort of get used to the way people live here, like if you're a guy, you start saying, "Why not do gangs? Instead of just sitting around, why not break into cars, sell drugs, get money in the house, just to provide for my family?"

And if you're a girl, you can get dependent on a man to bring in the money, and what if he dies? Go on welfare? I don't think that's a way of living.

I just finished high school, and I hope to go to university and study psychology. But right now my granny can't afford to send me. When she stopped selling drugs, the struggle really began. Twelve of us live in one house, and we live off my aunt's small salary and my granny's pension. There are times when at the end of the month we have to borrow money to pay for food.

But I have faith that I can make it out of here somehow. I've been attending a multiracial church for four years, and it's really helped me

Although she hopes to leave Westbury, Nithinia feels firmly rooted to the community. "If I do leave, I would feel a responsibility to come back and be a role model," she says. "Deep in my heart, I know I should take care of the people of Westbury. They're my people."

appreciate who I am. Through meeting whites there, I've seen that they can also make mistakes and that it's no use looking up to them. They're just the same; it's only the color, the hair, and the eyes that are different. And by getting to know blacks, I've realized that being black is a blessing, not a curse. Now when I hear Coloureds being racist, I reprimand them: "Now why are you putting blacks down? You're just as black as they are!"

I've learned to be proud to be a Coloured and to just be myself. I feel comfortable and confident with who I am. I decided a few years ago that it's my choice, that I can be angry at the whole world for the situation I've grown up in and be as messed up as everyone else, or I can start living and planning my future. I have a rich heritage, with both black and white in me, and I feel I can be an important part of the South African picture.

*The Land Act of 1913 is a prime example of the unequal distribution of land that has characterized South Africa's history. The act put aside 93 percent of the country's most arable land for white farmers and allowed Africans, who made up roughly 75 percent of the population, to own land only in the dry, overpopulated areas that remained. This forced many Africans to work on white farms, where they lived in small shacks beside the elaborate houses of their employers.*

*Nineteen-year-old Nomfundo Mhlana comes from a family that for several generations has worked for white farmers near Grootfontein in the Karoo, a vast expanse of flatland in the heart of South Africa.*

## BREAKING THE CHAIN
# Nomfundo Mhlana

I GREW UP on a white person's farm, where my father worked with the sheep in the fields and my mother cleaned the white person's house. My parents never even got a whole day off; they worked all 365 days of the year.

When I was small, I saw the bad way the whites treated my parents. When the farmers went to work, for example, they wanted my mom to take care of their babies. My mother and the white babies began to love each other—when my mother was playing with the baby, the baby would laugh—but when the babies got older, their parents would tell them, "This is a black, and she is working for us. She is

not like us." They didn't really see us as the same kind of human beings.

My mother was not friends with the white woman. I think the white lady liked my mom when she was working, but not other times. She gave her an Afrikaans name, Rosie, even though her real name is Nofozile. The whites knew that name, but they said they couldn't call her that because they couldn't say the name correctly.

As a child I felt bad about being black. When I saw the way our parents worked for the whites, I thought the whites were superior to us and that their white skin made them rich. I would look at the color of my skin and then look at the whites' color, and I would think, I wish I was white.

The white farmers that Nomfundo's parents work for live in this house. "Whites don't know us just because they have us working on their farms; few whites really know how we live."

▨ Nomfundo often helps her mother prepare meals in their three-room house. "We can live like this because we always have, but my parents would like to live in a bigger house."

Growing up on that farm, I didn't go to school until I was ten years old. The whites discouraged my brother and me from going to school because they were worried that we would get some knowledge and then want change. If I went to school, maybe I'd never come back and work in the farm kitchen.

So when I was small, I was learning at home and playing. My brother and I played with the white kids, but not as equals. If we were playing hard and hitting each other, I couldn't hit the white. I could call the children by their names, except if they were bigger than me. Then I called them *klein baas* [little boss]. The white children had

Nomfundo often helps her younger sister with her homework. "I am the oldest child, and my name means 'We are educated,'" she says. "So when I am finished studying I want to help my parents send the younger ones to school."

things I did not have; they had cars that worked with batteries and dolls that cried when you put them down.

We lived far from where the whites lived because the whites didn't want the noise from the black workers. I always wanted to go inside the "big house" because I could see outside there were grasses and flowers, so I thought that the inside of the house would be very interesting. But I was never allowed to go into the house because the whites thought that if I came in there, my shoes would make the house dirty or I would steal something. The whites knew that the blacks didn't have the things that they had, so they didn't trust the black workers. They would always keep a list of their sheep, for example, because they thought their black workers would steal one.

I went inside the big house for the first time when I was fourteen years old, when I came to talk with my mother in the kitchen. I was afraid the whites would chase me out, but I went in anyway. When I saw videos and TV and the rugs on the ground, I was angry. I thought, Why doesn't my home look like this? How could the whites have so many things and so many rooms in their house but my parents have nothing?

Now that Mandela is president, I think our society is more equal, but I also think whites still have apartheid in their hearts. They pay workers more because the democratic government says they must and because they're afraid of the law. But they still think they are better than us. We now live on a different farm than when I was a child, and my parents still have to call the whites *baas.* They still don't pay workers enough money. My parents have six children, and they would like to live in a nice house, but they only have enough money for food.

But I do have hope that some whites are changing their minds. The whites on the farm now will come into our house and drink some tea with my mother. They also have a daughter who is nineteen, like me, and we are friends. When she comes to ride horses, she greets me, and when I have something I don't know at school, I go to ask her, and she helps me. I'm now going to a school that was started by white farmers'

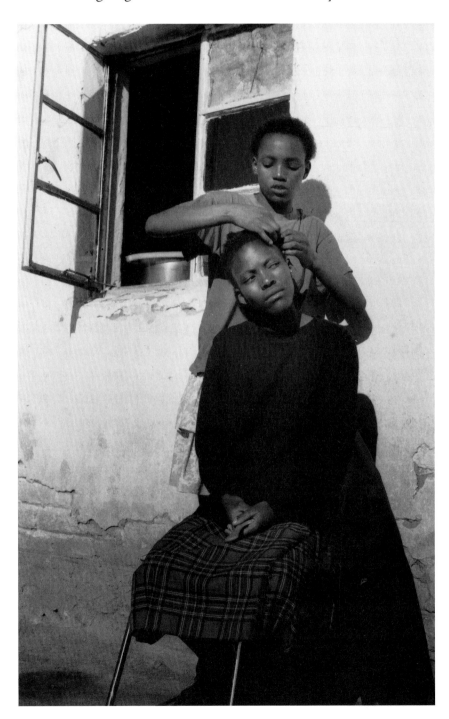

▽ Despite the difficulties in her life, Nomfundo is proud of who she is. "The whites have money, but I don't want to live like them. I am proud to be black." Here her friend Nowewes styles her hair outside the family's home.

wives, for children on the farms like me. The farmers at our place think it's okay that my brother and I are in this school, and they say that education is the best thing to have. In fact, they came to a party when the school first opened.

I will not work on the farm like my parents. They were illiterate and living in the times of apartheid, and working on the farm was all they could do. But my education will give me an advantage; it will help me get better jobs than they could. I want to have a career in social work because I love to talk to children and I don't like to see them being abused. I know that I won't make that much money as a social worker, but I hope that I will make enough to buy a house and let my family live there with me. Then they won't have to work on the farm anymore. My parents worked hard to allow me to go to school, and I must make them proud.

When I was small, I was jealous of whites; I wanted to be like them. But now I feel hope that I will have a bright future, and I am proud to be black. When I meet a white person who gives me respect and treats me like an equal, I treat him the way he treats me, but that does not mean I wish to be like him. I wish to be just like I am.

*Denied access to decent education, arable land, and well-paying jobs under apartheid, most black South Africans had to adopt innovative ways of finding money. For some, this meant leaving their homes and families in rural areas in search of jobs in mines, factories, or white people's houses in the city. This left many black children to fend for themselves.*

*Seventeen-year-old Michael Njova grew up amid poverty and was abandoned by his mother at the age of nine. By ten he had turned to crime to survive. He now lives in Kids Haven, an orphanage outside Johannesburg, in Benoni, funded by both the government and private donors.*

## BACK FROM NOWHERE
# Michael Njova

I GREW UP IN A RURAL AREA in Transkei with my granny and grandfather. My father ran away when I was born, and my mother had to leave and go to Johannesburg to find work because in Transkei there was nothing. She would send money back to help us, but I grew up thinking my granny was my mother.

I lived with my grandparents and my three cousins in a round hut with four rooms and a thatched roof. It took me a half hour to get to school if I ran and maybe one hour if I walked. I would take my grandfather's cows from the hut to the pasture before school, and after school I would bring them back. After that my grandfather and I would do the garden. It was nice in Transkei. I had friends, and on

Saturdays we would go swimming at the dam while we watched the cows.

But then my grandparents died. My mother came back for the funeral, and she said, "Now you must come with me to Johannesburg." At first I said, "No, you're not my mom," but when she showed me photos of me and her when I was a baby, I finally had to believe she was my mother.

When I got to Joburg, I was feeling happy; it was the first time I'd seen big buildings like that. My mother tried to put me in school, but I didn't know English because I had only been speaking Xhosa in

◥ After resisting it initially, Michael now enjoys living at Kids Haven, especially playing soccer after school with his roommates. "At first I got into so many fights, but then I began to understand that we are all here for our problems—he came like me, I came like him."

Transkei. So when she'd go to work to clean at a health clinic, I would stay home and watch TV.

Then my mother lost her job. She told me that she couldn't feed me but that I could stay with a friend of hers in Soweto while she looked for work. "Then I'll come and take you back to Transkei," she said.

I stayed with that friend and went to school in Soweto, but things were difficult. The lady told me, "Your mother is not paying me any money, so you must work for food."

I said, "How can I work? I'm only nine years old." But I worked anyway. I planted nice flowers next to their house like my grandfather taught me.

She just said, "That's all?"

Then the lady said I had to stop going to school. She told me, "How can I pay for your school when you're not my child?"

I remember I started crying. I said to that lady, "You must tell my mom to come get me."

She said, "I phoned, but I can't find your mom."

I wondered why my mother ever took me from Transkei. I wished I'd never left there.

So I decided to run away. I took a plastic bag with a few clothes, and I just took a train. I didn't know where I was going. When I got off, I saw that I had ended up back in Johannesburg. I went into the city, and I looked for my mom. But I was nervous, and I couldn't find the flat she and I had lived in. Then I ran into this kid I had seen on the train. He said, "Where do you stay?"

I said, "Nowhere."

He told me I could live with him and his friends on the street. He said they begged money from people and then bought food together.

I said, "Okay, I'll stay with you guys."

We were seven boys, and we slept on the sidewalk next to the grocery store on old beds. They showed me how to beg. They became good friends.

After a while the older boys said, "If you want more money, you must take the bag from the person." At first I said, "No, it's wrong." At my home in Transkei the people didn't teach me how to steal. But the group gave me a knife and forced me to do it. They were the big boys, and we small boys always had to listen to them. If I had said no, they would have said I couldn't be in the group, and then I wouldn't feel as safe on the streets. So I grabbed a purse from this lady, and my friends said, "Well done, you can run fast." It made me feel good that my friends liked what I did. I felt proud of myself, like, yeah, I'm a man now.

The second time I tried to steal, the lady and I saw each other in the eyes, so when I went to take the purse, she rolled it up and held it tight in her hand. Then she screamed and held me by my jacket, so I took the knife out and stabbed her. She fell over, bleeding. But I don't think she died because I stabbed her in the right way, in the ribs.

After that lady, I kept stealing and stabbing. We would mostly go for women, women who were walking scared. Maybe I stabbed sixteen or seventeen people. Maybe some of them died. But I really didn't want to kill anyone. I believed in God when I was in Transkei, but when I got to the streets, I started doing bad things. I started inhaling glue, smoking *dagga* [marijuana] and Mandrax [Quaaludes]. When I smoked the Mandrax, I'd think, I'm a man, it's giving me power to steal. Sometimes I wanted the drug so badly that I'd get a headache if I didn't smoke it. I might steal a cellular phone from someone, then sell it and buy Mandrax with the money. My friends made me feel it was okay, and I didn't think about my mother. I forgot about her and the past.

✉ Michael recently returned to school in Wattville, a township near Kids Haven, after his four years on the streets. "The first day, I didn't have a friend, it was me alone, the oldest. But I'm clever at school, so now they accept me."

Soon I got into trouble with the police. One time I saw a lady walking with her purse hanging, so I ran and took it from her. But the police saw me, and they let their police dog after me. He held me down by my leg so that I couldn't run. When they got there, they told me, "You can't go to jail; you're still young." So they beat me up, there on the street, kicking me hard with their boots and knocking out my front teeth. When I woke up, I was hurting all over and lying in my own blood.

▼ As one of the older boys at Kids Haven, Michael likes to help look after the younger children. "I have learned that when someone says show him love, you must show him you care about him, you must show him your spirit."

After I'd been on the streets for four years, a traffic cop caught me begging and said, "Where do you stay?"

I said, "Nowhere. I stay in the street."

He said, "Okay, I know of a place to sleep called Kids Haven." Then he took me there.

When I got to Kids Haven, I just thought, I'm going to run away from this place. I didn't like the other kids; I was just into my drugs. But then I saw the people there were inviting me to stay, giving me all the food I wanted and washing my clothes for me. It made me feel good that I didn't have to beg or steal, but I wasn't sure it was real. I was like, why are these people acting like my parents, wanting me to act straight? I just stayed alone, watching.

But after a while I decided the people there really did care for me. I made some friends, and we would watch videos together and do favors for each other. The big boys said to me, "Drugs are not good for you. You must leave the drugs." On the street no person did these things for me.

So I decided to stay at Kids Haven, and then I had to go to school.

▼ Michael practices karate twice a week at a local training center, where he earned a green belt. He recently won a gold medal at a national competition in Cape Town. "The street taught me how to use weapons, but now I am learning to use my body for self-defense."

⬎ Despite his struggles, Michael feels the past is behind him. "If you know me from 1997, then you go away and come back after five years, I will have kept the promise that I will not do criminal things. Even if I'm struggling, I'll find another way. I will not take."

I had missed so much school that they put me into Standard Two [fourth grade], even though I was fourteen years old. The first day I was afraid the children would laugh at me because I was so much bigger than them. Sometimes they teased me about being a "street child" and said I had no parents. At first I wanted to fight with them, but instead I just told the teacher. On the streets I learned violence, but now I was trying to go back to the way I was before I came to Johannesburg.

Now I do very well at school, and my favorite subject is accounting. When my teacher leaves the class, I say to the other children, "Come, I'll help you." People at Kids Haven have helped me, so I help others.

I want to do good in school because of my future. Black people have more chances than they did before. I want to be a pilot so that I can make money. If I get money, I'd like to make another home for street children. Mandela is trying to help these children, and I think in ten years there'll be less of them. Kids must not stay like I did on the street, struggling for so many years. The street kills people; it confuses and kills your mind; it kills everything you knew.

I know the street is not inside me anymore. Before, when I would see someone walking with a purse, I would think, There's big money, I must take it. But now I don't even think about it. When I see other street kids, they try to invite me to go back, but I say, "No, I don't want it," and sometimes I tell them to come to Kids Haven. I want to tell those kids my story because it will help them see they can change.

When I go into town these days, I'm always looking for my mother. I know her; in my eyes I can see her picture. If I see her, I will run straight to her and hug her. I used to blame her for leaving me; I felt like she threw me away. But now I just want to enjoy life with her and love her. I want to show my mother who I am now.

*From 1950 to 1990 between thirty thousand and sixty thousand South Africans left the country and went into exile. Even in exile these activists and their families were not always safe. In search of activists' whereabouts, police would intimidate and interrogate those family members who had stayed behind in South Africa, including old men, old women, and small children. South African death squads, manned by members of the police and military, would cross borders to detain or kill known activists.*

*In 1991, when the government finally lifted the ban on anti-apartheid organizations, most exiles returned home to South Africa.*

*Sixteen-year-old Vuyiswa Mbambisa is the child of ANC activists. She grew up in several foreign countries as an exile before coming home to Soweto.*

## COMING HOME

# Vuyiswa Mbambisa

I'M SOUTH AFRICAN, but I was born in Angola. My mother left South Africa when she was nineteen years old because she was an activist for the ANC, and she felt South Africa wasn't safe for her anymore. Everyone knew the apartheid government was torturing and detaining people who fought against it.

She made many sacrifices in leaving. She left behind her only son, Xolani, and the whole Mbambisa family. There was the risk that she'd never return to see her family or that she'd never manage to escape to where she wanted to go.

My father was also in the ANC and an exile in Angola. But I never knew him. When I was still a baby, he snuck back from Angola into

✦ Vuyiswa's extended family, including her grandmother, nieces, and nephews, lives in four different houses in Soweto, and she spends time with all of them. "The houses are for everybody; you're always welcome."

South Africa for a political meeting. The police heard about it and came and shot everybody, including my father.

My mother left South Africa to get a better life for herself, but that didn't mean she left the struggle. As an exile she could spread the word to the world that South Africa needed help. She went through military training in Angola and even Russia for the ANC's army, called *Umkhonto we Sizwe* [Spear of the Nation] and then worked at the ANC offices in Tanzania and Zimbabwe.

Even in exile my mom was afraid the South African security forces might follow her. She wouldn't allow me to come to the ANC offices where she worked because of the possibility that they might be bombed. She always told me not to talk to strangers.

I spent seven and a half years in Tanzania, living in a huge ANC camp in a community of South African exiles. For me it wasn't a hardship. The ANC gave us everything we needed: schools to learn at, houses to live in, and food for every household. It was like a small town where everybody knew each other.

But I also began to realize that my home and relatives were really in South Africa. At school they taught us that the reason we were in exile was the political situation in South Africa. There was a feeling that the struggle wouldn't go on forever and that one day we would return. Our parents and teachers tried to preserve the culture they'd left back home; we'd learn traditional South African dances, and we'd have ceremonies to pay tribute to heroes like Mandela, who had been arrested. I thought someday we'd have a big tribute and then go back to South Africa and be with our true brothers and sisters.

The older I got, the more I began to feel I was South African and nothing else. Even though I spoke Swahili and English [the languages of Tanzania], when my mom and I would walk in the streets, people would stop and tell us, "You're not from here; you're South African." Tanzanians called us *Mkimbizi,* which in Swahili is like "runaways." Some kids would tease me; they'd say, "Don't forget that you don't belong. You should go back home."

I remember I began to tell my mom, "Let's just go home to South Africa, where all of the Mbambisas and ancestors are. I want to be like everyone else." For me, going home was simple; it was just packing my bags and living with my grandma. But she'd say, "It's not that easy. It's not safe. The enemy is still there looking for us." She knew that the police had her name and that they had been coming to my grandmother's house in Soweto and asking where she was.

But my mom had to find a solution because she couldn't take my begging anymore. I think she finally understood that South Africa was where I belonged. She decided that it wasn't safe for her yet but that I could drive down with a family friend she could trust. I was sad to leave my mom because for so long I was the only family she had and

 Vuyiswa hopes to study business management after she graduates from high school. "I don't like things that come on a silver platter."

she was the only family I had. But I also thought, I've spent my whole life with you and now I want to go home. It made it easier to leave because she promised me she'd return when it was safe for her.

When my mom's friend and I got to the Zimbabwe–South Africa border, I was excited. I knew South Africa was just over there. But I was also scared because the police looked just like I'd imagined them—big white guys—and somehow I hated them. My mother had organized a false passport for me with a new name, Refiloe, and she prepared me for the questions they might ask at the border. "You're Refiloe and no one else. Don't change it, no matter what they say to you." Still, I felt as though the police could tell that I wasn't really Refiloe, and I was waiting for somebody to say, "What's your real name?"

But nothing happened. We made it through and arrived in Soweto at night. Outside my family's house my heart was beating fast. I was nervous because I didn't know how they would see me. I went inside where the whole family was waiting anxiously, and they started hugging me and crying. I saw this guy in the corner, and I thought, Wow, so this is my brother, Xolani. We were standing there staring at each other, and then we said hi and looked the other way. Finally we kissed and hugged, but for me it was like kissing a stranger! Something just felt right in that house, though. I finally had an older brother to look up to and someone to call Granny.

The next morning I got to see Soweto, and I was like, wow, this isn't what I had in mind. The kids were just so different from me; even though I never felt like I was rich when I was in exile, compared to many people in Soweto, I had a lot. I'd gone to multiracial schools, lived in big houses, and had almost everything I'd needed; they'd grown up isolated under apartheid and lived in little houses with toilets outside. They played in dirty streets with torn shirts and without shoes. Even though I'd studied about the inequality in South Africa, it was still surprising that people were living this way. I felt really out of place, so when I went outside, I'd just sit on the pavement and watch the other kids play.

School was also difficult. I was new, and everyone was talking about this girl who spoke English and Swahili. When I would try to speak Zulu like them, they would say, "Why does she speak so funny?" behind my back. A lot of the students thought I was high on myself; they had this perception that people from exile were privileged, that they had everything. "Oh, she's not from here," they would say. The teachers thought I was the brightest kid in class and that I should be an example. I know I also made enemies because of that.

It was really frustrating for me, because I didn't consider myself an immigrant. I was South African; I was just different, that's all. I just wanted the students to see me for who I was and not for what I had or how I spoke. I'd stand up for myself. I'd tell them, "We weren't in exile just to live a good life but to serve the ANC! I thought you people were supposed to support me!"

Still, they made me feel like a snob. It made me sit down and think maybe I really was one. I felt like, Hey, what's wrong with me? Am I really that different? I guess at some stage I had an identity crisis. I even developed this fake South African accent. I really began to think, I don't belong here.

During those times I missed my mother so much. She was the one person I could really be free with and who could always understand me. Finally, after Mandela was released from prison, she told me it was safe for her to return. When she came, I was so happy; it was like everything I'd dreamed of. My grandparents, my uncles, my brother, my mother, this is what I always wanted, the whole family together.

That was three years ago, and since then things have changed a lot. One year after my mother came back, she had a baby, named Themba, with a man she'd met in exile. Four months after she gave birth, she

▼ Vuyiswa's boyfriend, Tebogo, has been an important source of support since she returned from exile. "We've known each other for a long time. He understands my past, and he knows that sometimes others don't."

died of breast cancer. Two years after that my brother, Xolani, was killed in Soweto by a gangster who stole cars, sold drugs, and terrorized people in the township.

After my mother and brother died, I felt alone, but Themba is giving me the strength to go on. Although he and I may not share the same father, he's my mother's

When her mother died, Vuyiswa knew she would have to play the role of mother to her younger brother. "I've got to be strong for Themba," she says. "This is what my mother would have done."

child, he's my blood; I've got to raise him like she would have. I hope to be a successful businesswoman some day, so that I can provide for him like my mother did for us. I'm confident of my leadership skills, and I've learned that I can move past any hurdle.

I think if my mom could see me now, she would be proud of me, because the one thing she always told me was, "Don't let anything hold you back." I really think she and Xolani are around in some way, watching over me. I think when they passed, they knew I would make it.

My future is now for me and Themba; no one's going to stand in my way. Some people might think this is selfish, but I really don't care. I feel at home in South Africa now; I don't feel like an outsider anymore. I used to worry about what people thought of me, but now I understand what my grandmother meant when she used to tell me, "You don't need to change yourself. Just be who you are."

*To prevent white South Africans from realizing the full extent of its brutalities, the apartheid government closely controlled the information that flowed through the country. The question of how much whites actually knew about the atrocities and what they could have done to prevent them is still a subject of great debate. Many whites are now coming to terms with what happened during those years and are dealing with feelings of guilt about the privileges they enjoyed at the expense of their fellow citizens.*

*Sixteen-year-old Mark Abrahamson has grown up with his parents amid the tree-lined avenues and well-manicured houses of Rondebosch, a formerly all-white suburb of Cape Town.*

## REDISCOVERING THE NATION
# Mark Abrahamson

I OFTEN THINK TO MYSELF, I'm just so lucky to have been on this end of the whole apartheid system, lucky to have been brought into the world which I was born into. Around here we've got television, we've got two cars in the garage, we're linked to the Internet, we've got the hi-fi system. What would have happened if I had been on the other side? Would I still be the same kind of guy?

The majority of South Africans were oppressed during the time of my upbringing, but I was in a very protected environment and was kept away from the violence and the atrocities that were being committed. I think a lot of people outside South Africa have this perception that it was so violent that someone was getting shot around every

⬚ Mark often plays the piano for his parents in his family's living room. "The piano represents for me a kind of place where I can just be alone with myself, and it gives me a way of expressing my feelings."

corner, but it wasn't like that in my area. I've never seen a man killed before, even though just twenty kilometers away in the townships, young kids were being subjected to some *oke* [guy] walking into their house and gunning their parents down.

There were just such strong barriers between our two environments. As a kid I remember being at parks in our area and thinking to myself, Now why is that black person there? He shouldn't be there. It wasn't because I had anything against that person; that was just the normal way it was. If you look at Cape Town, it's quite remarkable: You've got a relatively affluent core center, and right next to it, really right over here, you've got a lot of poverty and unhappiness in the townships. But it didn't seem like these problems were right here in Cape Town; it seemed very distant, almost as if it was in another African country somewhere.

We weren't just sheltered; there was also an active hiding of the truth, propaganda, by the apartheid government. They knew that if we were able to analyze the true situation, sooner or later we would have come to the conclusion that it was wrong. The government controlled the television stations, for example, and the news became a joke after a while because it was so propagandist. If there was any violence in the townships, it was blamed on African forces fighting each other and not on white government intervention, which is what it was.

You also didn't really hear about the ANC. Whenever you did, it was through the news, "these people are messing up our land" kind of thing. And I hadn't seen pictures of Mandela, because you weren't allowed to have a picture of him anywhere around. He was made out to be a scary, violent character. "If he ever comes out," the government told us, "it will be the end of South Africa; we'll be thrown into civil war." I remember when I finally saw him released from prison on TV, it consciously came to mind: Why'd they put that funny old man in prison for so long? What could he have done?

In school, too, we weren't being told the real picture of South Africa. In the private school I attended, the government told the teachers what textbook to work from and what to teach. Certain books, like African literature, were just not allowed, and if teachers were caught teaching them in a class, they would be fined or put in prison. I remember reading Rudyard Kipling's books about African animals, but that's not really African literature, is it? It was almost like we could've been at a school in England.

I think I picked up on the racial situation quite young, but the whole process of assessing the situation and then feeling guilty is something which I've had to come to terms with much more recently. I don't know what I would've done if I was in my twenties at the height of apartheid. I don't know if I would've actually stood up and said, "I think it's completely wrong, and this is what I'm going to do about it."

But things have changed. We weren't told the truth for so long, but now we're hearing it all. We're starting to hear about the brutal attacks on people, to see pictures like the one of three policemen with their feet on a black man that they killed like it's a trophy. I've been shocked by what's come out, but I think it's necessary to hear it. What hap-

◤ Mark has gone to private schools his whole life. "I've been fortunate to get an education that's as good as it gets. Most black people have just not had these opportunities."

pened in our past is a wound. If we don't first put antiseptic on the wound, if we don't dig up our skeletons, literally and figuratively, it's never going to heal properly.

There's an age of rediscovery in South Africa at the moment, of finding out what's really out there, of getting to know everyone who is living here and consciously trying to live in harmony. We're the generation that's the bridge from the previous South Africa to a new one. Therefore I think it's crucial to become involved in this transformation, so that you have the sense of actually making a difference.

At my school I'm very involved in an organization called Interact, which focuses on community work. On Freedom Day [a national holiday commemorating the country's first democratic elections] this year there was a walk organized through all the townships, just to make us more aware of the city. Interact made it public to our school. I was very interested because I hadn't spent a long stretch of time in a township or really seen what was going on there. You can see things on television, but to actually be there and meet the people, reality kind of hits you.

So I went on the walk, and I got to see at close quarters what you normally just see from the road. We had to walk through a lot of really bad conditions. We even saw this one squatter community built over a rubbish dump. It was eye-opening because where we live around here, it's fairly clean. Walking through these places, I thought to myself, The only reason I'm not here is because of my skin color, which I didn't even choose. I also noticed that most of the people in the townships were quite friendly, happy people. I was expecting a lot more anger and irritation, like, "Why are you walking here?" But they actually wanted to show us around.

There's a fear now, especially among the more paranoid whites, that we're moving from a white supremacy to a black one, that black people are going to come knocking on our door, saying, "We're gonna divide your house in two." But that isn't what's happening. It seems there's this incredible feeling of forgiveness on the part of black people. It's like, "You know these white people have been terrible to us, but we're just going to show them that we're not made of the same stuff." I think we must be quite thankful for this atmosphere because as far as I'm concerned, black people have every right to turn the whole thing around and say, "Three hundred years we've been under this oppression, now it's your turn for the next three hundred."

Some white people are leaving South Africa, but I have no intention of doing so. I think if I was to be scooped up and put in Europe or

Mark and his friends like to eat lunch and see movies at the Waterfront, a huge seaside mall in Cape Town. "We live a very Westernized existence; we've had all the modern conveniences."

Mark spends a lot of time composing music at his computer. "I've written quite a lot of music, and most of it has been Western because that's what we're used to," he says. "But now there's a lot of African music being played, and I've written one piece that is consciously African. It's part of rediscovering where I come from."

America, I would be able to survive, but I would be very homesick for South Africa. Not many people have the privilege to be living in a country that is changing so rapidly, and I feel quite proud of my land, and I know that I belong here. I see our future being a positive one. I would like to be able to look back on my youth and say to myself, I was, even in a small way, somehow part of this success.

*Soweto, ten miles from Johannesburg, is South Africa's largest African township. It became a focal point of black resistance on June 16, 1976, when the apartheid government tried to introduce Afrikaans as the medium of instruction in African schools. Students in Soweto, infuriated by the thought of learning in the language of apartheid, organized a march to the local soccer stadium for a rally. When the students reached a police roadblock, police officers opened fire and killed several marchers.*

*The march and subsequent deaths sparked the Soweto Uprisings, which spread to townships throughout the country and resulted in seven hundred deaths by October 1977. Ninety percent of those who died were under twenty-three years of age. Thousands of young people were arrested, and about twelve thousand fled the country in exile.*

*Eighteen-year-old Bandile Mashinini's older brother, Tsietsi, was one of the principal organizers of the June 16 march.*

## STRUGGLE IN THE BLOOD
# Bandile Mashinini

◥ I'M THE LAST BORN of thirteen children. Several of my older brothers were very involved with the anti-apartheid movement, and three of them ended up going into exile.

No one really knows exactly when my brothers left. It's not like they wanted it to be a mystery; they did it for safety reasons. If they'd announced when they were leaving and where they were going, I have no doubt it would have reached the police station in a second. You just didn't know who to trust in those days.

My brother Tsietsi was the police's number one fugitive. He had been one of those responsible for arranging the June 16 march. The way things were, you couldn't start a series of events like the Soweto

Uprisings and still live a normal life. Once the authorities knew you were capable of stirring up the whole township in one day like that, once your name was shouted out as a hero a few times, either you left the country or faced imprisonment.

That's when the police started busting down the doors of our house, looking for Tsietsi, like three times a day. I remember one time

▨ Bandile has a lot of friends in Pimville, the section of Soweto where the Mashininis live. "We notice the way Americans dress, with baggy jeans and tops that hang out, and I dress like that as well," he says. "But I'm also growing dreads right now, because I want to make a statement about African pride."

▼ Bandile likes to talk politics, even when chatting with friends on a slow Saturday afternoon on a Soweto street corner. "I've always had political arguments over almost everything. The Mashininis have political blood."

I was playing outside and I saw three police vans pull up. I ran between the cops, and by the time I found my mom to tell her, four guns were pointed at both of our heads—rifles, shotguns, pistols, the works. Other times you'd hear noise outside, then boom, they were in the house, shaking you up on the bed. "Get up, *kaffir*, let's see who you are." They'd have this big flashlight in your face, guns pointing at you. They'd search under everything, on top of everything, behind everything; they'd ransack the whole place.

Because my brothers were political, we had ANC T-shirts and documents in our house that in the eyes of the law were incriminating. We'd put them inside the coal stove and cover them up. But some-

▼ Bandile is the youngest student in his public administration class but a frequent contributor. "I want to go into politics, so I'm studying now to figure out what particular battles I want to fight."

times we'd sleep in those shirts, and a few nights when the cops came, it was like, "Wake up! Here's another terrorist wearing Mandela. In the van, buddy." They'd take people in my house to prison for a whole night's interrogation on why they were wearing a political T-shirt.

My mother was also arrested and spent seven months in solitary confinement. One of my brothers in exile tried to make contact with her, and somehow the police found out about it. The charge was aiding terrorists, helping them escape, which she did, but one has to ask—who were the terrorists, really?

This kind of harassment went on from when I was born until the late eighties. At first it was very scary; I'd be shaken up by the whole thing. But later I got used to it and saw it as part of our life. In fact, I'd even think, Once in a while we ought to give those fools tea, they visit us so often. I mean, they would kick down the door in 1984 and ask where Tsietsi was, even though he'd left in the seventies. It was like, hell, you know he's not in the country, so why are you looking for him here?

As a kid I didn't really understand the deep meaning of the politics that my family was following. I knew there were good guys and bad guys. The ANC were the good guys; cops, the bad guys. I was a noisy little character, yelling, *"Amandla!"* ["Power to us!"], and that kind of thing because I could sense that if I belonged to this family, it was in the blood to view things politically. That's what we're known for.

Now that I'm older, I realize that my brothers, filling the better part of their days with ANC training camps and the cause, lost a part of their lives that is associated with just being young. When we celebrated holidays at home, when everyone was sharing and having a good time, my brothers were in the field somewhere, forced out of their own country by white people and living like some sort of creatures on the run, never able to settle down.

Two of my brothers finally came home in the early nineties, but

☑ Bandile sometimes visits the grave of his brother Tsietsi. "Tsietsi contributed toward making the new South Africa possible. Now we must take it from here."

Tsietsi never came back. He died in 1990 while still living as an exile in Guinea. There's a lot of controversy and suspicion surrounding his death. There was a story that he died of a nervous breakdown, and I know he had a disease of some sort that affected his nerves and led to violent episodes. But we also know he died with bruises all over his face and very fresh injuries. I don't think there was ever a postmortem performed on him, so no one really knows what happened.

We brought Tsietsi's body back to South Africa and buried him in a cemetery outside Soweto. Later there was a special memorial tombstone built at his grave, and there was a big unveiling. You see, people still identify Tsietsi as a hero. If a person recognizes me as a Mashinini, even now they make a lot of noise, like, "I used to go to school with your brother!" His name still carries a lot of power, and some Africanist organizations even shout it in their slogans today.

Tsietsi, together with my other brothers and the rest of their generation, helped achieve the society we have now. Unfortunately Tsietsi did not get to enjoy the new South Africa like the rest of us. Now that it's here, we ought to make the most of it; we ought to be a generation of South Africans who live their lives to the fullest and have fun. But just because the "big struggle" is seen to be over doesn't mean we should party the rest of our lives; we should take off from where the previous generation left us.

To me that means getting a job in the new government so that I can be part of the actual improvement of our nation. We have a new constitution, and it's a great foundation, but it's still only ink on paper. I want to make sure we build well on top of it. This is going to be hard work, but then I'd be a dreamer if I thought I'd never have to make any sacrifices. I can never imagine there's an end to the struggle.

*There are some rural areas in South Africa where life is more about continuity than change. Most people in these areas live in thatched mud huts and keep a few cows, sheep, goats, and chickens. Most grow their own fruits and vegetables.*

*Fifteen-year-old Pfano Takalani has grown up in a small village in Venda, a lush, hilly region in the northeast corner of South Africa. His family has ruled Mukula village and those around it since 1911. Pfano's father was the third chief in the lineage and had four wives and twenty-six children. In 1993 his father died, and Pfano's brother, the eldest son of the first wife, was installed as the chief.*

## THE SAME OLD ROAD
# Pfano Takalani

I KNOW WHAT APARTHEID was, because I was taught about it at school, but we didn't experience it here. I only know of two instances when I've spoken to a white person—once to a German missionary who lived around here and the second time when two guys were looking for directions out to the main road.

We live a very traditional life here in this part of Venda. Because I am the son of the chief, I have always been expected to follow the traditional rites. When I was younger, there were times when we were grouped as boys, and the elders, especially women, would tell us what they expected from a boy my age. For example, if I'm wearing a cap

◤ Pfano must show respect to his elder brother, Chief Takalani, by sitting below him. "My brother attends university, but otherwise the system of ruling is still the same. He has to look after the welfare of all of the community."

and I meet an elder, I have to take off the cap because it's our tradition to show respect to people older than me. And I must always greet the elderly first. Also, when I'm being sent somewhere by a stranger, as long as I know that the stranger is from the village, I'm supposed to do what he says. If he sends me to a shop or to fetch water, I'm not to challenge the instructions.

I was also taught by my elders the tradition of the reed dance. We make our own reeds by breaking off hollow branches, and then, with the help of the elders, we cut them at different lengths so that we each make different sounds. We then blow into these reeds while we dance. We do the dance about thirty times a year. Sometimes when a chief has been installed in another area, we are invited and we perform the dance.

When my brother calls a serious meeting, we children are expected to summon people. We bring out the big drum and make sounds that instruct people that there is a meeting. We have older boys who show us how to hit, and then we're tested to make sure we're doing it right.

◤ To keep in top form, Pfano and some of his twenty-five brothers and sisters often get together to practice drumming and dancing. "There are elderly people who train us in the different kinds of sounds for each dance," he says.

To make sure the message reaches every corner of the village, sometimes we have to go out and tell people about the meeting in person. The elders who are close to the chief often use this tradition to put us to a test. They estimate a safe distance for our age, and then we are sent to run. I think the last time I had to run six kilometers alone to fetch a man who was too stubborn to come. I was very tired!

In my village, if I have done something naughty and it affects another family, the other family is called into the chief's place, and he hears their story. Then I'm called in and get cross-questioned, and a judgment is made. If there's anything that has to be repaid to the other family, like if I tore another boy's shirt, the elders from my family will repay them, but I'll be in for it. Most of the time I'll get a hiding, but other times I'll just be given some extra work like wheelbarrow carrying or smearing the huts with different kinds of mud to make them look beautiful.

I think that even if I was not in the royal family, I would still try to follow our rules. Many young people who go to the cities and then return to our village now follow Western ideas. When they are sent somewhere by an elder, they just argue about the distance or why they aren't getting paid. The elder person will then not want to teach them Venda rituals or to give guidance on how to grow up. If these traditions are lost, we will lose a lot of human dignity.

There are some things we have in our villages and in our culture that they just don't have outside. Here you can have big pieces of property and even grow some bit of fruits. Here you can have lots of wealth in terms of goats, sheep, and cattle. You cannot own those in town. And there's a lot more good here than in those areas, like the respect and general laws of human behavior. We don't have so much drinking, fighting, crime, and killing.

It's also nicer here if you are poor, because you can look for help from the community. Sometimes the chief will call a poor family to

 Pfano's relatives all live in the royal compound, including his 105-year-old great-grandmother. "I am trained to take decisions from all of the mothers around me."

come and work at a specific task at the royal *kraal* [compound]. Normally poor people do respond to such calls, and after they do the work, the chief kills one of his cows and feeds them. This makes sure nobody is too poor in the community.

But sometimes I do wish I was born in the city. I feel sad when I hear that in Johannesburg there are new houses being built with electricity and running water, whereas around here we've never observed any progress and no improvement in our schools. People here are still struggling: We have one water tap providing for a wide area, most people do not have electricity, and we still have dusty roads.

✉ There is no running water in Pfano's village. "The water system is still the same old water system," he says as he fills water jugs for his family from the closest tap.

I blame the government for not improving things. I know about the changes that happened in South Africa in 1994. Most of the people in this community voted for the ANC because they thought there would be improvements, but there haven't been any changes. The old road is still the same old road. There was once a plan where the poorest in the village would be called to the local clinic to come and collect bags of corn, just after elections, but soon it disappeared. I don't expect many changes in the future because when I grew up it was like this, and it's still like this now. If Mandela was president, or de Klerk [the last president under the apartheid government], it wouldn't make any difference.

I've been into the city a few times, but when I'm older, I'd like to live here and do what I can to help my community. Personally I don't feel like we are backward. When you grow up with tradition, you get so used to it you can't afford to give it up. I want to be a nurse at our clinic so that I can save lives. I'd also like to help my brother with his decision making and problem solving as chief, so that we can work with the government to bring us better roads and water. Maybe when I'm an elder, I'll even sit on my brother's royal council because we need to have continuity. I want the Takalanis to have power here for a long time.

*South Africa's black youth played an instrumental role in the fight against apartheid. Frustrated with the government's system of Bantu Education, whereby schools were segregated and blacks given an inferior education, these young people spearheaded boycotts of schools and sometimes advocated violent action against the apartheid state. "Liberation before education!" became their rallying cry.*

*Now that the common enemy of apartheid has been destroyed, these young activists face the task of redefining themselves in South Africa's new democracy.*

*Seventeen-year-old Lebogang Maile is one such activist and the president of the Congress of South African Students (COSAS).*

## DEFENDING DEMOCRACY
## Lebogang Maile

I STARTED TO GET INVOLVED in political activism as a young teenager because my father and brother were activists, and they inspired me. I was also affected by the inequalities I saw around me. Under apartheid the people who received quality education were white, because if whites were educated, they would be able to always oppress us. White schools were well resourced, while our classrooms were crowded, our teachers poorly trained.

I was aware from a young age that we were oppressed by whites, that the white person was the enemy. I joined organizations that said, "One settler, one bullet!" and "Drive white people to the sea!" In

those days black students saw their schools as apartheid structures and would call "stayaways," where we all stayed away from school, both teachers and students. Some students began to break school windows, take electric wires out, and even burn the schools down as institutions of the enemy.

◤ Lebo is known among his friends for his activism. "It is important for me to understand what decisions are being taken on my behalf, and then affect those decisions."

We were in a war situation back then. We destroyed schools because there was nothing else we could do; it was the demand of the conditions. But now our society has changed. Today we are living in a society which is democratic. It's a very exciting time to be a young person in South Africa because we have more opportunities than the generations of the past. I have freedom of movement; I can speak whatever I want to speak; I have a right to join student organizations; schools are now accessible to all; there is no longer official discrimination.

This means that the role of the activist has changed. We need to remain militant as students, but now that democracy has come we need militancy in another form, one of pressuring government to address issues that affect us, not of throwing stones and burning schools. We must play the role of constructive watchdogs, confronting the government when it's necessary and supplementing it at the same time. This is part of the idea that "the people shall govern." We must come with facts; we must debate issues. To advance our democratic gains, we must take up the challenge of nation building.

One place to do this is in our schools. Although the present government is trying to equalize education between whites and blacks, we are still far from equality. You can still see the differences: Whites have school buses and computers, but at my school our phones don't even work. The government needs to take those resources and redirect them to disadvantaged schools.

But at the same time, the government is trying. It is building new schools and developing a new curriculum. It's going to be a long process because it inherited a disaster from apartheid. Students can help by supplementing the government's attempt, taking a lead in reconstructing the schools, just as our predecessors took the lead in destroying them previously.

This is why I joined COSAS. I believe we need to have a strong student movement to bring about education transformation. I want to

◤ Lebo goes to the COSAS office almost every day after school. He and his colleagues often work there till late in the evening. "Some days I have school, then there is a meeting at five, then I go home, eat, and sleep, and then tomorrow it starts again."

be part of bringing equality to our schools, of addressing issues like racism, sexism, and discrimination. I thought that if I was vocal about this issue, people would see that the matter was serious. Now I see that through my position I can educate, mobilize, and organize many students because sometimes democracy depends on numbers.

As president I am trying to show students that there is a necessity for us as citizens of South Africa to be equal. I am going to private

◥ Lebo has lived his whole life in the African township of Alexandra, located in Johannesburg. "There are different people with different beliefs in Alexandra," he says. "When we meet we share ideas, and then I develop as a person."

schools, where the white people have money, and I am telling those students, "Join COSAS. Be part of us; come with ideas of how we can bring equality to our schools." For real progress and transformation to be reality, I believe South Africans must be together, united in the process. This land belongs to all those who live in it, black and white. Personally I forgive whites for what they did, and, in fact, I am prepared to work with them.

But the question is, Are whites recognizing us or welcoming us as their brothers? Do they see the importance of us getting educated, of us becoming equal with them? They use the labor of our parents, and

▧ Lebo is involved in several student organizations, such as his high school's student representative council. "I want to see South Africa being transformed, and my part in COSAS alone won't make that happen," he says. "My involvement in many different political structures is part of my education and activism."

now they need to plow back and help us. The ministers of education alone can't bring about equality. The rich whites know about the conditions in black schools, and now they have a responsibility to ensure that there is educational equality.

Although our endeavor to reconcile may now be having some hiccups, I think the fact that we see our president, Nelson Mandela, shaking hands with F. W. de Klerk, who led the people who oppressed us, shows that we can attain reconciliation. In the past people were tortured, their rights were infringed, but now is the time to come together and look forward to a new society, one that is democratic, nonracial, nonsexist and that is prosperous.

I want to see everyone being equal in South Africa, but I worry about the reluctance of the young people in the country. Now that everyone is liberated, many don't see the importance of defending that democracy. When a decision is being taken by the government, most young people don't even bother to think about how it will affect them. They will all go to festivals, but if we have an event to improve the conditions in our schools, they won't come. They see politics as a waste of time.

It frustrates me to see other young people being apathetic because their ignorance is a danger to our democracy. If they're ignorant, one wonders what will happen in ten years to come. We'll be the future adults; therefore we need to develop leaders and begin the process of shaping our future. But how can we do this while most of the youth don't care what is happening in our country and internationally?

But I also believe there is a small number of progressive young people who will protect the democracy we have and ensure that we raise the consciousness of others about the importance of participating in politics. There is this perception that politics is a dirty game, but I don't agree. Politics is about our lives.

The Truth and Reconciliation Commission (TRC) was established in 1995 to help South Africans heal the wounds of apartheid. The TRC invites victims and perpetrators of human rights violations to speak in a public forum, to express the pain, bitterness, or regret that has been with them for so many years.

Many of the stories coming to the TRC originate in KwaZulu Natal, one area most affected by the violence that accompanied apartheid. There a complicated battle emerged between two predominantly black political groups, the ANC and the Inkatha Freedom Party (IFP). But what appeared to be black-on-black violence was actually initiated and fueled by the apartheid government; white policemen and soldiers supplied support or weapons to both sides, simply to continue the cycle of violence.

Fourteen-year-old Nonhlanhla Mavundla testified at a special TRC hearing for children. She lives in Khayelisha, a small village nestled among rolling green hills where hundreds of survivors of violence from throughout KwaZulu Natal have resettled to make new lives for themselves.

## HEALING THROUGH REVEALING

# Nonhlanhla Mavundla

▼ I WAS TRAUMATIZED before I had come to know what was happening in the world. I was eight years old when the conflicts arose between the IFP and the ANC in the rural area where I lived, and many people were killed. This kind of violence stays in your mind; you keep on thinking about it.

Before the violence came, we were all living together peacefully in our village. We used to get along as neighbors, help each other, support each other during funerals or anything we were confronting as a community. You could walk around at night, and it was a lively place to dwell in.

This changed when the violence started. Even families became

separated because some relatives would side with the ANC side, and others with the IFP. There just came a feeling that you could not trust anybody. I could not even play with other children next door because some of their families were belonging to the opposite side of the conflict. The village began to look desolate. The fun had stopped; there was no one playing on the streets.

My home was built near a playground where political leaders from one group liked to punish people from the other group. They whipped them with *sjamboks* [whiplike sticks made out of animal hide] and killed some people by putting motor tires around their necks and then burning them, using petrol. The old people would say to us children, "Get inside! Don't look!" but I would hear the screaming. I was really confused because I could not understand seeing people killing each other when we all looked alike.

We lost trust in the police. They would come as peacemakers, but then they would kill people. I remember one time I was watching TV at home, and I saw police vans passing, driving down to my uncle's place. They wanted him to be a witness for some killings that happened, but he refused to talk. I ran out and told my aunt that there were police going for my uncle, but when she got to him, the police had already shot him in the foot. They then put him into their van, where, we were told, they went about torturing him until they killed him, twisting his neck and burning him with cigarettes.

My parents used to try and protect us from this violence; when things got really hot, they'd put us away with relatives. When I'd come back, my parents would say, "People came to attack us, you nearly found us dead, but we ran and escaped and hid somewhere." I was aware during those times that it was death or life, and every time I was going back home, I would keep on thinking, Are my parents still alive?

One time when I was away, my parents arrived at our relatives' house with nothing in hand, except a few pieces of clothing. They had run

A special person in Nonhlanhla's healing has been Sister Elizabeth, a nurse who gave her counseling and a shoulder to cry on. "The nurses helped me in relating my feelings," she says. "Now life seems peaceful."

away from home because a group of men from Inkatha had burned down our house. We were staying in an area that was mainly ANC, and they put fire on each and every home there, not just mine alone. Everything was burned.

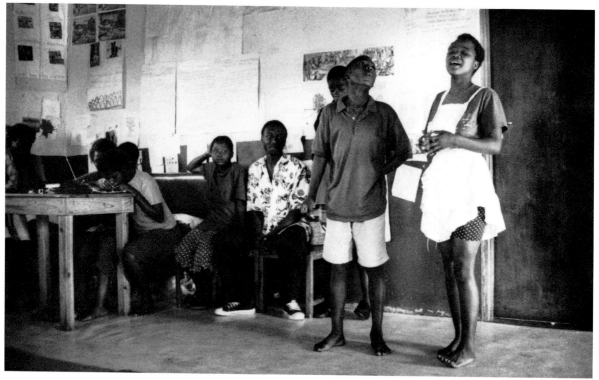

▨ Singing is one of Nonhlanhla's favorite activities. "If I feel sad, I feel comforted after I sing." On weekends, she performs with other survivors of violence whom she knows from a youth group.

This made life hard because we had to start over. My family had stayed in that area for a long time, for generations. Even the grandmothers got married there. It was our home, but now we had nowhere to go.

We moved nine times after the fire; we were always running away. The whole area was full of violence; there was no way of choosing a new place. Things were like that all over. We became separated from some of our family during this time, and we still don't know where some of them are. It hurts me because when there is a feasting day, there is no way of getting all of us together. I keep thinking maybe this uncle or that aunt is going to come, but then the celebration is over without me seeing them. I don't know how we will meet again.

But now there has been a change in the behavior of people. They are no longer doing the violence they used to do. My life is becoming better and better, though it hasn't reached the happiness that I had before the violence started. After all the moving, we've managed to get a two-room house to live in, at a place called Khayelisha, which means "new home." There I am staying near kids who have also experienced bad things, even though we come from different places and political groups. I like living close to them because we've been able to share our experiences with each other. I am also back in school now, after three years without it.

There came an announcement a few months ago that all those children who had suffered in the violence could bring up their

Nonhlanhla is grateful to be back in school after three years without it. "I don't fear that anything else bad will happen to me because I'm praying, and I don't think God will leave me now."

✎ Because her house has no running water, Nonhlanhla brushes her teeth outside. "There is no work for my parents, so our standard of living is still very low."

statements to the Truth and Reconciliation Commission. I wanted to go because I felt it should be known that I was traumatized and was a survivor. There were so many things that were hidden, and the TRC is making sure that everything comes out, that people get the truth. Maybe then people will not commit the violence they've done before.

I went to the TRC in Durban with the other children from Khayelisha, but I also mixed and played with kids from other areas. It was healing to see that other people had problems, too, some even more than mine. I also think there are many more children who have stories like mine who did not get to speak, so we call ourselves lucky that we were included in the hearings.

It helped me to speak there. Usually the people who go before the TRC look hurt when they are talking, but afterward, because they have told many other people, they look relieved. This is how I felt: By

✍ Despite the difficulties in her life, Nonhlanhla feels optimistic about the future. "Children were affected by violence just like adults, and we still have a long way to go," she says. "But we will make things better, we will arrange things in a different way than our parents."

talking about what happened, I've begun to forget it. And I know that if I never talked about it, maybe today I would be involved with drugs, trying to get some help or comfort from them.

Now when other children survivors are gathered, I can tell them, "We all experienced violence in some way, but now let's continue with our lives and be ready to learn whatever will be helpful, day in and day out."

*Although most South Africans are only just beginning to adjust to the realities of the post-apartheid era, some people, places, and institutions have been embracing tolerance and multiculturalism for years. As systematic as it was, even apartheid couldn't always stop the human desire for harmony.*

*Thirteen-year-old Lavendhri Pillay has been lucky enough to grow up in such settings. While schools in the rest of the country are just beginning to integrate, her school, Sacred Heart, has been open to all races since the mid-1970s. And while black people are just beginning to move into the formerly all-white areas of towns and cities, Lavendhri has grown up in Yeoville, a diverse and vibrant area of Johannesburg well-known for its racial tolerance.*

## TOWARD A RAINBOW NATION
## Lavendhri Pillay

PEOPLE ASK ME all the time, "What are you?" I say I'm South African. Then they say, "No-no-no, but what *are* you?" When I was small, I was always told that my great-grandfather came from India to pick sugarcane, but my family doesn't really have ties to India anymore. So I say, "I was born here, I've lived here my whole life, I don't know anything else, so I'm South African."

I've grown up different from a lot of other teenagers in South Africa because I've been subjected to all different races and different kinds of people. I'm a really lucky person.

Since I was seven, I've gone to school at Sacred Heart, where everybody's completely mixed. We've got Coloured, black, British,

history of our country, we'll be able to know what was wrong about what people did, and not to do it again.

But at the same time, I think we should be making a future. We can't just get stuck in one place, always staying on the same subject. My generation was lucky enough to not have been part of the struggle against apartheid, to have been only young when elections happened; we've grown up in other times when race is no longer governed by law, no longer an obligation. That gives us the freedom to address anything. We need to learn how to move on, to look at other issues that affect us, to try and do better, more different things. Our generation is more open-minded than our parents', and this makes me optimistic about this country. Since it's up to us, I think we can change things.

*it will be us*
*steel-taut to fetch freedom*
*and—*
*we will tell freedom*
*we are no more strangers now.*

*Mongane Wally Serote*
*from the poem "No More Strangers"*

**Tim McKee** lived in South Africa for four years, witnessing the final years of apartheid and Nelson Mandela's historic victory while teaching history and English at a multiracial high school in Johannesburg. After studying for his master's degree in journalism at the University of Missouri, he returned to South Africa in 1996 to work with his former students and to launch the school's first student newspaper. His experiences with his students sparked the creation of this book. A graduate of Princeton University, Tim McKee now lives in northern California.

**Anne Blackshaw**, an anti-apartheid activist in the 1980s, first visited South Africa in 1992, where she began documenting the lives of South Africans with her camera. She then worked as a women's and civil rights advocate in the California legislature. She returned to South Africa in 1996 to serve as an organizer and counselor for People Opposing Women Abuse in Johannesburg. There she continued her work as a photographer, focusing on women and young people. This book was her way of capturing some of the vibrant spirit propelling change in South Africa. Anne Blackshaw now lives in northern California.